SO MANY BLESSINGS
ALONG THE WAY
– A MEMOIR

By

Georgia Bell Floyd Kennedy

Library of Congress Cataloging-in-Publications Data
So Many Blessings Along The Way - A Memoir/Georgia Kennedy.
ISBN 979-8-218-19622-6

1. Kennedy, Georgia Bell Floyd. 2. Survival 3. Spiritual Growth 4. Personal Growth
5. Encouragement

See, I am sending an angel ahead of you
to guard you along the way
and to bring you to the place I have prepared.
Exodus 23:20 (NIV)

DEDICATION

This book is dedicated with much love and affection to my dear and wonderful sister-mother Pearline Floyd Gill who has always encouraged and inspired me to do "what thus saith the Lord" and contributed greatly to making me who I am today. You will never be forgotten.

IN LOVING MEMORY OF MY SIBLINGS:

MARTHA LEE DICKSON 1927 – 1981
FANNIE FLOYD 1946 – 1989
EMMA LEE FLOYD 1936 – 1991
ROSE COLE 1931 – 2002
PEARLINE GILL 1929 – 2016
JOHN FLOYD, JR. 1938 - 2022

ACKNOWLEDGMENT

I cannot express enough thanks to my daughter, Pamela Kennedy Barnett, for the management and completion of this project. I offer my sincere appreciation for the time and effort you dedicated to it. Just know that "your labor is not in vain" (1 Cor 15:58, paraphrased).

Table of Contents

INTRODUCTION

Tell me, what are the chances of talking with my niece, Ethel Dickson McCombs, about my desire to write a book about two of my sisters and then she mentions it to her friend and coworker, Patricia Hemphill. Patricia then tells her that she has a newspaper article that is 55 years old that was published on August 5, 1957, about my sister Fannie Ann, who is the sister that I had planned to write about and who was the inspiration for the book!

I realize that this was one of So Many Blessings Along The Way that could happen in only one in a million chances, and it can only be credited to the favor and grace of God! Miss Hemphill said that she obtained the article from the home of a school teacher named Mary E. Massey who taught at Lando Elementary School and had passed away. Her home was being cleaned out when they came across the article. Patricia had heard about my sister through Ethel. Miss Hemphill gave the article to Ethel who then gave it to me to use for my book.

I must say that without a doubt, I have had So Many Blessings Along The Way for which I cannot explain, but I can only give God the glory for it all. My story is a remarkable one, and I believe that it should be shared.

So Many Blessings Along The Way- A Memoir is my story of being raised by my loving and caring sister who unselfishly gave of herself to make me into who I am today. Also, I shared about leaving my family to follow a dream in hopes of a better life, and I can truly say that I have lived my dream. I hope you will enjoy my story and be encouraged and inspired to trust and believe God for your divine appointments in life. The journey has truly been great. To God be the glory for the things He has done!

After readers have finished this memoir, my hope is that you will realize that although life sometimes has a way of altering your dreams, you must persevere. You will discover in the pursuit of your dreams, that there are *So Many Blessings Along The Way*!

Let me share my journey with you. Let's go!

CHAPTER ONE

The Floyd Family

My earliest memories of our family take me back to our two-room house with a large front porch out in the country. We had a well in the backyard where we would go to draw water. Our household included Daddy (John Floyd, Sr.), Lena Mae ("Philly"), Emma Lee, John Jr., Fannie Ann and me.

In the summertime, Fannie Ann and I would get up early so that we could go out by the big oak tree in the front yard where we used to make mud pies and plait grass like it was hair. Daddy worked on the farm harvesting hay which he would throw into the barn. June and I would play in it. When Daddy would come in from the field, I would jump onto the back of the wagon and ride down to the barn. Philly used to say that I was the only one who would get on that wagon and ride to the barn with him.

We were out there in the country - just us. There were no other children around to play with, and I don't remember us ever going anywhere. We didn't start going to church or anywhere else until we moved in with my sister Pearl. In the winter since it was cold, we stayed in the house most of the time and we would play with our baby dolls and look out the window all day. Philly, Emma and

June would gather the wood and place it inside the house behind the stove after Daddy cut it up.

We had our own cow that Daddy would milk, and he would bring the milk inside to churn and make butter for cooking. We would drink the milk with our cornbread that Philly made. We ate peaches and cornbread, and cornbread with pinto beans. We also raised our own chickens; we would behead them and prepare them for Sunday dinner. Oh, that was the best chicken gravy. We also had hogs that he would butcher and hang them up in the barn so that they could dry out and we would have cured ham.

I recall that Daddy had a mule and wagon, and he would go to town to get flour, sugar and whatever we needed; he would always take June with him. None of the rest of us were ever able to go with him. Sometimes Daddy would go to visit his lady friend, Miss Belle. That was his little outlet away from us and work.

We were a very close-knit family. My sister Pearl would always come by to check on us to make sure we had what we needed and to ensure that we were okay. If any of us needed anything, we could always rely on my sister Pearl.

I never really knew much about my Mama because she died when I was about four years old, but I've been told that I look like her more than any of my other siblings. After Mama died, Daddy took care of the younger children which included Philly, Emma, June, Fannie Ann and me. The other three older children: Lee, Pearline, and Rose - had already left home.

In a little city called York, in York County, South Carolina, on Highway #5/Black Highway, about thirty miles south from the big city of Charlotte, North Carolina, there is now a school called Cotton Belt Elementary School that was built on the exact spot of land where I was born and raised on February 8, 1943. My name is Georgia Bell Floyd Kennedy, and I am the seventh child born to my parents, the late John Andy (Budjer) Floyd (b. 1898) and Mary Givens Floyd

(b. 1911). My father was a sharecropper and my mother stayed at home to care for my siblings and me.

> Sharecroppers rented small plots of land from landowners in return for a portion of their crop which was to be given to the landowner at the end of each year. Sharecropping enabled landowners to reestablish a labor force, while giving poor whites and freed Black people a means of subsistence. About two-thirds of sharecroppers were white, and one-third were Black.[1]

We lived in a tenant house that was located on Inman Farms which included several other tenant houses, peach orchards and a peach packing shed that was located directly across the street from where we lived - which remains to this day. I tried to work at that peach packing shed, but I couldn't do it because that peach fuzz had me itching all night long! But thank God, my sweet and dear sister, Pearline Gill, rescued me from that job. I don't think I would have survived if I had to work in that place another day. There were several other people who worked and raised their families out there during that time, and just about everybody was related to somebody in one way or another.

Twelve children were born to my parents while they lived on Inman Farms. They were oldest to youngest, Martha Lee (Lee), Pearline, Rosa Mae (Rose), Lena Mae (Philly), Emma Lee, John (June) Jr., Fannie Ann, me, and four other children who died when I was still a small child and of whom I really have no recollection. My sisters, Lena Mae and Fannie Ann, share the same birthday of January 26th.

Daddy farmed the land that we lived on and raised corn, cotton and wheat. He would get up very early in the morning to milk the cows and feed the horses and chickens and then go to the field to work the rest of the day. While Daddy was out working, the children were all at home taking care of each other and doing our daily chores like washing, ironing, cooking and cleaning. At that time, Philly and Emma did most of the cooking, cleaning and washing and taking care of me and Fannie Ann. After working, Daddy would come home, eat his supper that Emma and Philly had prepared and get ready for bed. I must give credit to Philly and Emma for making sure that our clothes were always washed, clean and neat. They took good care of us while Daddy was out working.

Daddy kept up this routine faithfully for a while until one morning, my brother-in-law, Dan Gill, came over from their house, which was not too far from our house on the Inman Farm, to bring Daddy the light bill like he always did. When he went in to call him, he did not answer. Apparently, he had died in his sleep. I was lying right beside him and didn't even know it. Oh, I was so heartbroken to know that he was gone, and I missed him so much! It was so unreal. I didn't know what to do. I was only about six years old when my Daddy died. All my memories of Daddy are good, especially when I remember all the special little things that he used to do for me. I always felt safe and protected when he was around. To me, he was the best father in the world, and I loved him so much. He was a man of medium height and slim build, a gentle and a very kind man. He took great care of everyone and clothed us as best he could despite the circumstances, especially after the loss of my Mama. I'm not sure of the exact date when my mother died, but from what I understand, it was sometime after the birth of Fannie Ann because she was so hurt and heartbroken because of her condition.

After Daddy passed away, Pearl took us home with her immediately. At Pearl's, we lived in a three-room house with two bedrooms. The household included Pearl's five children (Tootie, Sister, Nancy, JoAnn and Danny Boy), June, Fannie Ann and me. There were at least three or four to a bed. Pearl and Dan slept in the living room on a couch. Later, we were able to move to a bigger house that was owned by Roe Inman.

The owner of the farm where we were living at the time as well as a few of our relatives thought that it would be best to put my brother June, my sister Fannie Ann and me into an orphan home because we were not old enough to take care of ourselves and because of Fannie Ann's condition. At that time, many people didn't want to deal with the responsibility of caring for someone with a handicap or disability and would generally want to put them away and not want them to be seen. They probably thought that it would be too challenging and extraordinarily demanding for Pearl since she was already taking care of her four other children. However, my dear and wonderful sister, Pearline Gill, to whom I will be forever grateful, would not allow it. Not once did I ever see Pearl waver in her dedication and commitment to making sure that we were cared for and loved. I truly thank God every day that she did not listen to any of them! She was determined that we would not be separated. She was always so good to us and treated us like we were her own children.

This is my mother, Mary Givens Floyd

Me.

My sister, Rosa Mae (Rose) Floyd Cole

My sister, Emma Lee Floyd and her friend, Ed Thomason

Emma Lee

My sister, Lena Mae (Philly) Floyd

My brother, John ("June") Floyd

My sister, Fannie Ann Floyd

While living on the farm, Pearl worked for Ms. Cora Inman and her family who lived across the street next to the peach shed in what we used to call the "big house." Pearl washed, cooked and cleaned for them. When I was about ten years old, she took me to work for Mrs. Cora and Dr. Charles P. Roper, and this was my first job as a young girl. I would babysit and care for their two small children, Jane and Julia. I went to work there every day. Every weekday when I would get off that big yellow bus after school, I would take my books home and went straight to work until about five in the evening. When I got there, they always had a peanut butter sandwich and a Coca-Cola waiting for me to eat and drink. I really loved those Coca-Colas back then! That was such a treat for me all by myself. When I was done eating, I would take the children out to play, push them in the hammock, give them their supper, and then go home. On the weekends, I would fix their hair and get them dressed to go out and play for the day. I basically did whatever else they needed done. I was paid fifty cents a day every evening. I continued to take care of Jane and Julia until I moved to the city of York, and it was a pleasure to work for them because they were very nice and kind to me.

I would save my money and almost every Saturday, I would walk to the store that was close to our house to buy Fannie Ann and me some lollipops, tootsie rolls and a soda. I would have a bag full of stuff! We didn't tell anybody we had it, and we would go in the room and eat. Sometimes you could hear the bag rattling when trying to eat it by ourselves and hoping nobody would catch us doing it! We were so happy together; those were some happy times!

Sometimes on weekends, I would spend my money on my sisters, Philly and Emma, and me. We would get dressed up in the nicest outfits we had and grease our legs so that they would be shining. We would walk uptown to go to the dime store to buy stuff. Then we would hang out around town, watch people go by, and walk up and down the street until almost dark. Sometimes we would even go to the movies. After the movie was over, we would walk back home and talk about the good time we had that day. At other times, Philly, my brother June, and I would go to this juke joint called Clyde's that was owned by a man named Clyde Thompson on Saturday nights. Philly would dance and have a ball. I would only stand around and listen to the music because I wasn't a good dancer. My brother would make sure that nobody bothered me if I didn't want to talk to them. He was my bodyguard.

This is Jane (top) and Julia (bottom) Roper when they were small.
These are the children for whom I cared.

CHAPTER TWO

My Sister Pearl – Our Precious Jewel

My sister, Pearl, was a God-fearing woman who believed in going to church and taking all her children with her. Pearl was the best thing that ever happened to me! Her favorite scriptures were Psalm 23 and John 14:27b (KJV) – "Let not your heart be troubled." She loved to read the Bible, and she lived it as well. She used to keep a New Testament in her purse and many times you would see her pull it out and read it whenever she felt like it. She always spoke to us with comforting, heartfelt words. I can assure you that no matter what was going on, she always remained as steady as a rock! Her favorite songs were "Love Lifted Me", "You Can't Hide, Sinner" and, "This Little Light of Mine."

We used to walk about one or two miles to attend our home church, Fishing Creek Baptist Church, which is located on Spring Lake Road off Highway 321 in York. We did not have a car for transportation, so each Sunday, we faithfully walked to Sunday School and worship services. We seldom missed church, and we were always on time for ten a.m. Sunday School and eleven a.m. services. It took us about forty-five minutes to walk to church. Now, do you think I liked Sunday School after all that walking? No, I didn't! I didn't like it at all; no, not one bit! All I know is that it seemed like as soon as we were rested, it was time to walk back home, and we were already tired! And no, I didn't want to participate in Sunday School class at all because I was tired! Since Fannie Ann was not able to walk and she did not have a wheelchair at the time, Mr. C.W. Curry or Mrs. Virginia Byers would come by and pick her up, and then they would meet us at the church. Mr. C.W. Curry and Mrs. Virginia Byers were good friends of the family that attended church with us. Pearl was a member of Fishing Creek Baptist Church her entire life and served as a member of the Missionary Ministry and the Usher Board Ministry. Also, Pearl was a faithful member of the kitchen committee for many, many years.

My sister, Pearl, took me under her wings and taught me how to carry myself as a young woman and have respect for myself. She made the sacrifice to make sure that we all stayed together as a family no matter what, through thick and thin. She was committed unselfishly to our well-being. She never mistreated us; Pearl was always gentle and kind and never spoke harshly to any of us. She was the best mother anyone could ever have. She had an easy-going, calm strength about her and always said, "All we have in this world is each other, and we have to stick together," and we did. If anybody in the family had any problems, they would always go to Pearl for the answer. She made sure we had good manners and were always respectful. She saw to it that we never started eating without washing our hands and blessing our food. We were also taught to always kneel beside the bed and say our prayers and always thank God for another day.

For the most part, I never saw her angry without a just cause, and that was rare. You would have had to really show out badly to get her worked up!

In 1947 when Pearl was about eighteen years old, she married a man name Louis "Dan" Gill, and they were married for fifty-three years. They had eight children. All of Pearl's children took part in helping her to care for Fannie Ann after I left home. She was also blessed to have twenty-five grandchildren, forty-eight great-grandchildren, and ten great-great-grandchildren, and she truly loved taking care of them. If she was out of town for any amount of time, she would say, "I have to get back home to see about my grandchildren." She loved them so much.

My sister Pearl was my hero because she saved us from God knows what. She and her husband were sharecroppers and worked in the field picking cotton. I didn't like working out there in the hot sun. I couldn't wait for the sun to go down so we could go in the house. I was about nine years old when I started going out in the field to pick cotton. We had to carry those sacks on our backs, and we had to try to fill them up. I don't think I ever got one full! I told my sister that I would rather help to take care of her children and Fannie Ann and that I would cook and keep the house clean after school. So, my sister began to teach me how to cook on that old wood stove, how to add the wood, make a fire, and most of all how to keep food from burning and catching on fire. One day when she was showing me how to cook different things, her husband, Dan asked her, "Pearl, do that girl know what she doing?" and my sister replied, "Yes, she does."

Pearl was so thorough and patient in showing me exactly what I needed to know to become an excellent cook like she was. One of her favorite books of the Bible was Job. Pearl would proudly tell stories of her past and how she continued to endure life's trials and tribulations by being patient like Job in the Bible and how she was waiting on her change to come. If you were to ever ask her how she was doing, she would boldly and humbly tell you, "I'm holding on to God's unchanging hand." And she would often tell you as well, "I know a man named Jesus." She really had the patience of Job - more patience than I - for sure! She didn't mind telling others about her experiences because she felt joy in telling others about the mighty God she served.

Pearl was well-known for her great cooking skills and especially her creamed corn, sweet tea and stickies. Stickies are a type of cinnamon roll that are made from scratch that were wonderful to eat with warm milk. She was often called and well known as the "Stickie Queen" because there weren't many people around who could cook like her!

In the early 70s, Pearl experienced her dream when she was able to purchase a brand new four-bedroom home, which was her pride and joy. That home made it possible for her to do exactly what she loved to do and that was taking in and helping people whenever she saw the need to do so. And I tell you what, she did that her entire life. It was her calling, and she took so much pleasure in knowing that she was being a blessing to someone else. She had no problem giving, even if it was her last. She had such a loving and giving spirit and would always let you know that "We brought nothing in this world, and we will not take anything out with us when we leave" (1 Timothy 6:7, paraphrased).

Pearl never turned away anybody from coming to the house and staying if they wanted. All our cousins loved to come over and wanted to spend the night. We would all have to pile up in that little three-room house and everybody was sleeping everywhere. Sometimes I just wanted them to go home!

For as long as I can remember, Pearl always worked many jobs to provide for us and her family. She was highly respected by many of her past employers and co-workers. Her past employers included York Restaurant, Huntley's, Klear Knit of Clover, South Carolina, and the York School District. She worked for the Inman and Roper families for forty years. However, for some reason, she didn't seem to be busy enough because she managed to find the time to go back to school and get her high school diploma from the Adult Education Program in 1976. She was a phenomenal, awesome woman!

My Precious "Pearl"

Pearl and me

My sister, Pearline and my brother-in-law, Dan Gill

*My sister, Pearline, went back to school after raising her children and
graduated in May 1976 from the York Adult Education Program.*

Pearline with children for whom she cared

On June 13, 2005, an article was written about Pearl in The Herald in Rock Hill, South Carolina where she was featured on the front page in honor for her commitment and dedication to others in her community. The article was titled, "Supplying food and fellowship - York woman fills kids' stomach, hearts through program."

Pearl participated in the program year after year so that all the children in her neighborhood were fed.

Pearl's light continually shined bright, and she was always a beacon for others. She would always encourage people to look up when they were down and inspired them to move on when the way was dark. If you were wrong, she would be quick to tell you, "That's not nice!" "God doesn't like ugly," and, "Be Sweet." She was a humble servant of God who unselfishly and willingly gave of herself and her gifts. She was a blessing to me and countless others.

Sadly, my sister departed this life on March 2, 2016, and went home to be with the Lord. She did not live to see this completed work that was penned in her honor. Throughout all of life's adversities, we had sisterly love for each other, and we put God first. When God made my sister Pearl, He broke the mold, and I don't think I will ever know any other human being in my lifetime with so much love, patience and faith. I can say, without a doubt, that she "finished her course, she kept the faith." And another thing that I loved so much about Pearl was that whenever you left from visiting her, she would always speak the blessing upon you from Numbers 6:24-26 (NKJV) in the Bible: "The Lord bless you and keep you; The Lord make his face shine upon you, and be gracious to you; The Lord lift up His countenance upon you, And give you peace."

She would also let you know that she was keeping you in her prayers, and you could rest assured that she was praying for you! You could feel it.

I will always love and cherish my memory of her, and I thank God that He gave me a beautiful, rare and precious jewel. He gave me a "Pearl." She was the foundation and strength that gave me the chance of hope and love and started my journey toward a better life.

"Pearl"

CHAPTER THREE

A Whole New World for Georgia and Fannie Ann

About a year after Fannie Ann, June and I moved in with Pearl, she decided that I needed to be enrolled in school. I did not want to go to school, but my sister felt that it was the right thing to do, and she was always about doing the right thing. I was not happy about this at all and did not like it one bit! I had never been on a big yellow bus before, and it was such a very scary situation to me. Out in the country where we lived, there was nothing there but dogs, chickens, cows, horses, and us! I was not used to being around a lot of people other than my family. When I was with them, I always felt safe, secure and well-protected. But all of that was about to change.

When I started going to school, the new environment really made me feel so uncomfortable and out of place as a lot of the people seemed "uppity." I wanted to quit so badly. I was about seven years old when I started going. I really felt so out of place like I didn't belong there - especially since the other children came to school all dressed up in their nice clothes with ruffled socks and hair bows. Many of the children were not nice to me, and they said mean things about my clothes. They tried to make me feel bad about myself so many times that I can't even count. Oh, I was so miserable, and I hated it with a passion! I was sick to my stomach every day. What they didn't realize was that they had parents to provide all they needed and wanted, but I did not. I tried not to let my sister know how I felt about school, because she did everything that she could to make sure we were getting what we needed to make it in life, which also included a good education.

One day when I came home from school, she noticed that I was somewhat sad, and she asked why. After I told her what was going on, she told me, "Don't worry about those children at school because God loves you just like He loves those children, so just go and get a get a good education." She always knew how to give you an encouraging word to keep you going no matter what! Pearl had a soothing, calming way about her which I loved so much, and she made me feel like I, too, belonged there.

Although I had a strong desire to not go to school, I continued to endure it. One day my baby sister, Fannie, asked me what I was doing when I was doing my homework, trying to learn to read *Dick and Jane*. Oh my God, I will never forget how excited and tickled Fannie Ann would get when I would read, *See Spot Run*. And then she would say, "See him run," and laugh uncontrollably. *Dick & Jane* was the first book she learned to read by herself, and she could read it from front to back easily. That was one of her favorite parts in the book. She really loved reading *Dick and Jane*. That book was a real treasure to us back then, and we had so much fun reading it! The book *Dick and Jane* literally changed our lives forever. Pearl's decision to send me to school was the best thing she could have done for me and Fannie Ann!

From that day on, when I got off the school bus, I would take my books home and go straight to work. By the time I left there, it was nearly dark, and since we had no electricity I had to use a kerosene lamp to light the room so that I could see to work on my lessons from school. Then I would take time to teach Fannie Ann, get ready for bed and start all over again the next day. This routine continued for about four years, and Pearl would also help me with my lessons when I was not able to figure it out on my own. Pearl and I taught Fannie Ann all we could until I got to the fifth grade.

It was only because of Fannie Ann that I eventually began to like going to school, seeing that she enjoyed reading the books that I brought home from school so much. We never really had any books at home of our own. Fannie Ann would be anxiously waiting for me to come home so I could read to her and teach her how to read and write. She was always glad to see me get home because she waited patiently all day long for me to arrive. As soon as I would get in the house, she would be sitting there and she would say, "I'm ready." And sometimes I would be so tired, and I wanted to go straight to bed, but I just could not let her down because she was depending on me to help her learn. Although I would read a book to her only once or twice, somehow, she was able to take in and grasp everything that I taught her with such ease. She was more excited than I was about the books! Fannie Ann let me know that I needed to pass my grade so that she could get some new books to read! Good gracious, no rest for the weary!

Her enthusiasm and eagerness to learn helped me to push past what I was facing while going to school every day. It made me want to go and get all the information I could to take back to her each day. She just loved learning. Although my sister was handicapped, she was a very bright and intelligent individual who craved knowledge and was very eager to learn the things that I would teach her. Despite her limitations and her inability to walk, Fannie Ann was always a very cheerful and happy little girl. She was the love of my life.

Due to Fannie Ann's condition, there was a nurse/social worker, Mrs. Lucy Dunlap, who came to the house every other week to check on Fannie Ann's health. One day in 1957, when Fannie Ann was eleven years old, Mrs. Dunlap was there for her weekly visit, she noticed that Fannie Ann could read, and recognized a "potential to grow mentally," if not physically. She was so impressed that she contacted the school superintendent and brought Fannie Ann's case to the York School District Board Meeting. At the meeting, they voted to have a school-bound teacher come out twice a week on Tuesdays and Fridays to teach her at home. An article was placed in the August 5, 1957 Evening Herald, entitled "God Sorta Made Up To Fannie Ann With Bright Mind For Crippled Body" telling of her need to have a certified teacher to come to the house for two hours to teach her, and that the state of South Carolina was willing to pay for the tutoring. There were many inquiries and applications from persons interested in the "home-bound" teaching post. The superintendent approved the request and a second-grade teacher by the name of Mrs. Lee Taylor at Jefferson School was selected. Believe it or not, Fannie Ann was already reading on a fourth-grade level when Mrs. Taylor started coming out to homeschool her from what I had already taught her from reading to her after school, even though she had never been to school a day in her life.

A follow-up article entitled "Day To Remember" was written about Fannie Ann that shows Mrs. Taylor assisting her during one of her home visits and said that Fannie was probably the happiest child in York County because the biggest desire of her deprived young life had become a reality. Mrs. Taylor said that Fannie had been a bright pupil and her facility "in reading indicates she is ready for fourth grade work."

CHAPTER FOUR

My Ticket Out

On the following Sunday after that article was featured about Fannie Ann in the newspaper, we were sitting out on the front porch like we usually did, watching cars go by. We watched as a man drove up to the house in a very fine light blue Chevrolet with a black convertible top. When we saw him, all we could do was stare because his hair was processed and slicked back, he was dressed in a black suit with a crisp white shirt and black bowtie, and he had on some black and white wing-tipped shoes. Good gracious alive, that man was one of the sharpest men we had ever met or seen before! We had never really seen anybody like him. He reminded us of a celebrity – confident, classy, flashy, handsome, and I must say very, very well pleasing to the eye! He looked a lot like the R&B singer James Brown (literally). Fannie Ann and I sat there staring and asked each other, "Who is this man, where did he come from, where is he going, and who did he come to see out here??"

When he finally got out of the car, much to our surprise, he had in his hands some ice cream along with the newspaper article about Fannie Ann. He introduced himself as Hazel Gore Kennedy and said that he was looking for the child that was in the newspaper because he was so impressed with the young girl that he was interested in meeting her and wanted to see if he could do something for her! So, he found out where we lived and came out to the farm and brought her some ice cream. I tell you what, I could not have imagined in a million years how that one decision of my dear and darling sister, Pearl, to send me to school would have such a wonderfully awesome impact on us for our entire lives!

We really enjoyed meeting him that day. After that day, he never missed a week without coming out to the house to bring Fannie Ann something. I really think he didn't miss a week to come and see me too! He fell in love with me and Fannie Annie after he met us. He would cook food and bring it every week for the entire family, and he would always bring cake and ice cream, too. He took care of all of us. At first, I didn't really like him because I had never met a city guy like him before. But I tell you what, everybody in the city knew who he was; he was well-liked by just about everybody, and he had a great reputation. Hazel was always as sharp as a tack when he came out to see us. He was dressed to kill! I mean, talk about your heart skipping a beat and taking your breath away. That's what he did! He took my breath away.

Hazel and I eventually started going out, and I really enjoyed myself, too. One of the main reasons I enjoyed our time together was when we went out to the movies, I didn't have to share my popcorn like I did when I went to the movies with other dates! Also, I would get a meal that I didn't have to share either. Wow! That was a treat for me because when you have a large family, you had to always share just about everything.

Hazel when we first met him in 1957.
Wow, talk about making an impression!

When I started going out with Hazel, I didn't want to seem too anxious to go out with him, but I was. So, I played hard to get because my sister Philly told me to do so. Both my sisters would coach me on how to get together with him. Emma said, "Go on and talk to him because he will take good care of you like Mr. Ed does for me."

When he would come out to the farmhouse to see me, my sister would tell him, "She ain't here," and I would be right there in the house peeping out the window to see what he would do. He would get back in his car and drive out of the yard as fast as he could go. Oh gosh, we would laugh our heads off! But sure enough, a couple of hours later, he would come right back again looking for me. But I'll tell you what, we kept him on the run for a while! But eventually I gave in because he never seemed to get tired of coming back to look for me. Little did we know it, but Hazel was my ticket out into a whole new world of so many things I had never seen and done before.

That's the man!

Hazel would take me to his house and would cook for me. This was around 1959. He would come to pick me up and I would go to his house and help him strike matches for the top of a beautiful table that he was making. It was an extraordinary work of art. Although he only completed the sixth grade, I think, Hazel was very smart and was willing to learn how to do just about anything. He was a jack of all trades and could fix almost anything. He had many interests and hobbies and really loved to dance.

The table Hazel made from wooden match stems in 1959.

Hazel liked to go places and do things. On the weekends, he used to take me riding in his boat. I remember one time when we were getting ready to go boat riding on Lake Wylie, South Carolina, he put the boat in the water and had gone back to park the boat trailer. In the meantime, I was sitting in the boat looking in the mirror, combing my hair and not paying attention, then when I looked around, the next thing I knew - the boat had floated out into the water with just me in it! I was so scared because I didn't even know how to swim. Hazel told me what I needed to do to get back to the riverbank and guess what . . . you didn't see me looking in a mirror anymore while I was out in that boat! We had some good times together.

He had plenty of money (more than we ever had) when we went out, too. I really liked going with him to different places and seeing different things I had never seen before. We would go to different clubs in Rock Hill, Gastonia, and clubs in Charlotte like the Hi-Fi and the famous Excelsior Club which was located on Beatties Ford Road. We would go to Baltimore, Maryland to see his mother, Minnie Bryant Kennedy, his uncle, Roosevelt Bryant (wife Rebecca), and his aunt, Mamie Byers (husband Edward) and hang out with them almost all night. Those people liked to party all night long, but I didn't; I hated it! I didn't know anything about partying and drinking like that. I wanted food and all they wanted to do was drink. But his Aunt Becky, who didn't like to drink or party either, came to my rescue.

Hazel in 1965

Hazel and me with friends at the Hi-Fi Club in Charlotte.

I remember one time we were going to take a trip to Baltimore at the spur of the moment (long before the kids were born), and we didn't have any clothes with us, so we went shopping at the Sears that used to be in Uptown Charlotte on North Tryon Street. While we were shopping, I saw a dress in the window on the mannequin that I really liked.

"Try it on to see if you can wear it."

"Can I try something on that's in the window?"

"You sure can," and he told the salesperson to get it for me. When I tried it on, it was a perfect fit, and he bought it for me! Now that's one thing about Hazel, he liked to look good, and he always wanted me to look good, too. Hazel always knew how to really make you feel special and good about yourself. Oh, what a blessing he was to my life in so many ways.

Hazel truly made a difference in my life and was the best thing that ever happened to me and my family. Hazel loved and took care of my family like they were his own and that really meant a lot to me and was one of the special qualities that I loved most about him. He always tried to do whatever he could to provide for my family as well as for me and our children. He took very good care of my sister Pearl because he knew how much she meant to me. Hazel would do all he could to make sure that Pearl had whatever she wanted or needed, as well as her children.

My love and me in the dress from Sears

Hazel and me

Hazel and me at Atlantic Beach, South Carolina

CHAPTER FIVE

Fannie Ann—A Life Well Lived

When we moved my sister and her family into the city, it also made it possible for Fannie Ann to be able to attend Jefferson High School easily. The York Lions Club provided Fannie Ann with a wheelchair which made it possible for her to attend school physically. My sister Martha Lee's daughter, Martha Jane Floyd Sherer and my sister Emma Lee's son, Jimmy T. Floyd, would come and get Fannie Ann every day and push her to school in her wheelchair because the school was within walking distance.

There were so many people who didn't mind taking her on many excursions through town or wherever she wanted to go. She could always find somebody who was willing to push her where she wanted to go. Jimmy T. was also committed to making sure Fannie Ann had transportation when he got his license, and he would take her many places she needed to go as well. There were many people that had great attitudes about assisting Fannie in reaching her goals in life and were more than willing to help because we were family and we needed to stick together. Also, Fannie was a very confident and self-assured person, and she was very interesting, funny and delightful.

There was an article written on Thursday, June 2, 1966, in the Rock Hill Evening Herald which details Fannie Ann's graduation from high school. On that day, the district school superintendent described her as a "living symbol of courage, determination and cooperation." Fannie Ann described that day as the achievement of a goal she set a long time ago. Fifty seniors received their diplomas that night at Jefferson High School and Fannie Ann was one of them. Hazel and I bought Fannie Ann a brand-new wheelchair for her high school graduation gift. She was so thrilled and excited about getting it.

After Fannie Ann graduated from high school, she began processing income taxes at home. She was so proud of her accomplishment that she told Pearl that she could give the welfare people their money back because she could make her own money now. At the time right before I left, they were receiving $20 a month from welfare for both of us.

Fannie Ann—Her Busy Social Life

Fannie Ann had a very outgoing personality and loved to meet people and go places. She had always been around people and enjoyed all activities in which she could participate. She was very much involved in our family's home church, Fishing Creek Baptist Church. Fannie was an Adult Sunday School Teacher, a member of the Pastor's Aide Committee, the secretary for various organizations and a member of many other committees and auxiliaries. Fannie Ann would attend almost every revival that was going on when she could, and she would meet a lot of people during those meetings. She made herself well-known everywhere she went. Despite her small stature and inability to walk, she was a very active individual, and she never met any strangers. She was always willing to talk and would carry on a conversation for hours. She was a lot of fun!

Fannie Ann organized and held the first family reunion on the Floyds' side of the family, and we had a great time getting together with everybody on a happy occasion and not a sad one. She did all she could to make this happen. Normally, the only time that we would get together was during a funeral. I don't think we've had another reunion since then.

She participated in bid wiz card games on the weekends and was a great player. She enjoyed going to the beach and attending parties as well as participating in many other social events. Every year, she would make it a priority to come to Charlotte and spend the weekend to attend the Shrine Bowl of the Carolinas at Memorial Stadium, where the oldest high school football all-star game in the nation was held. Fannie Ann also became one of Hazel's best traveling buddies. Anytime he was going somewhere that I might not want to go, he did not hesitate to proudly take Fannie Ann as his date!

Fannie Ann playing bid wiz with friends

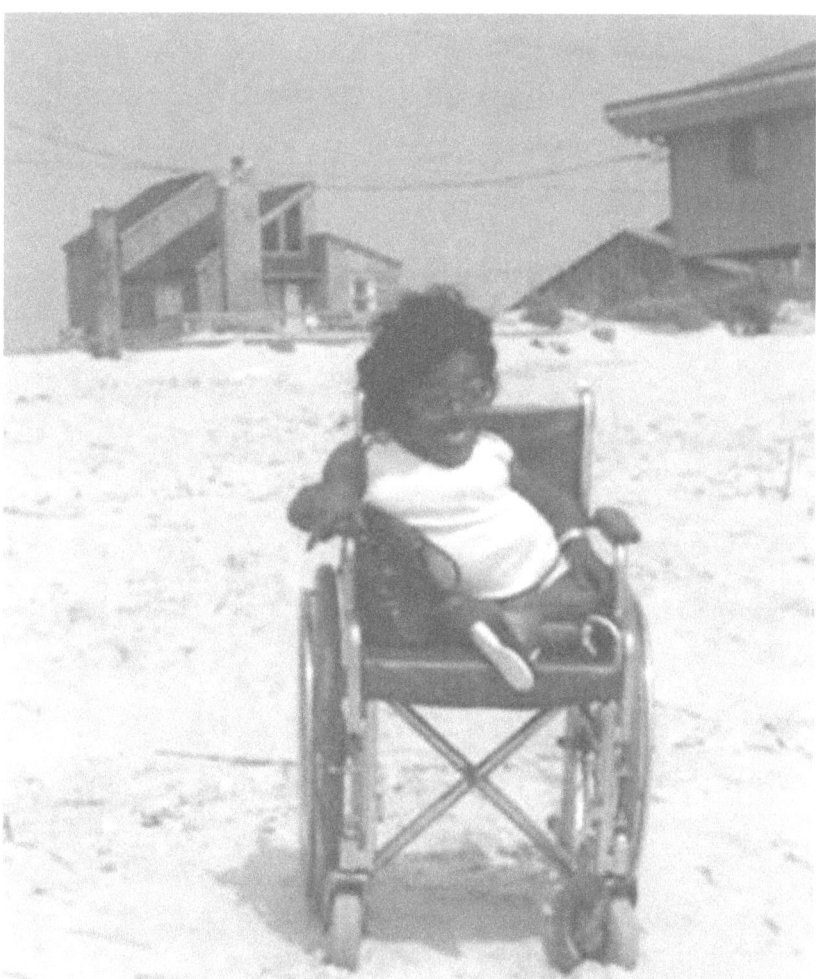

Fannie Ann hanging out at the beach, enjoying life

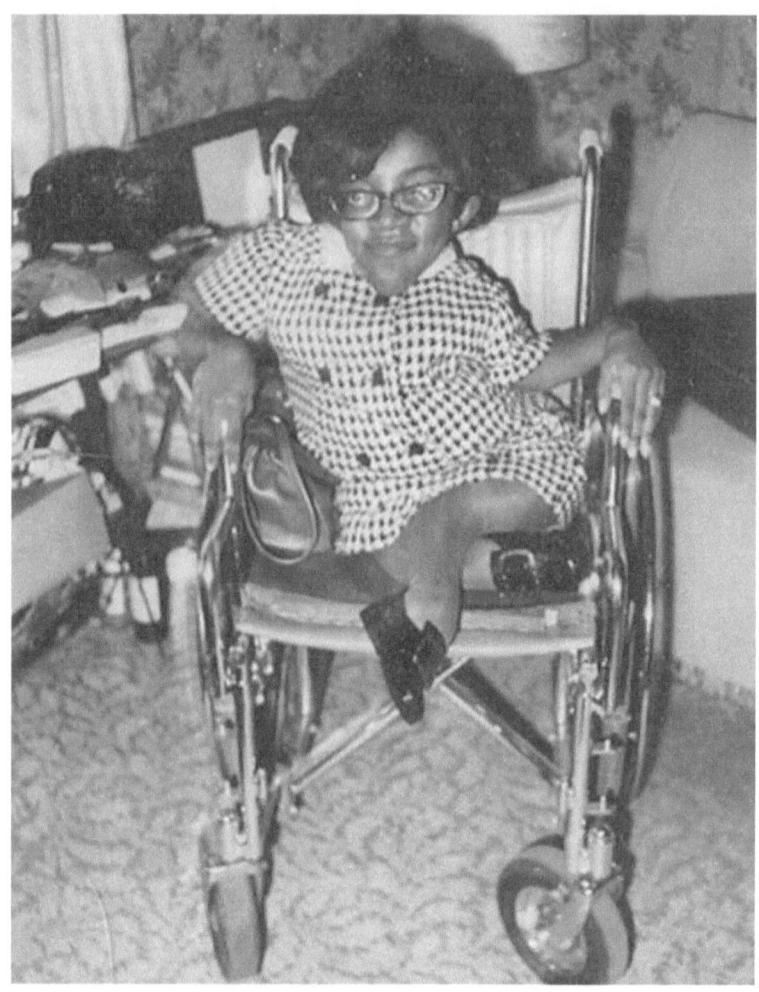

Fannie Ann getting ready to go out for the day

Fannie Ann Attends College

A couple years after graduating from high school, Fannie Ann decided that she wanted to attend college and chose to go to York Technical College located in Rock Hill, South Carolina. My nephew, Jimmy T. Floyd, would take her back and forth to school until she graduated along with her good friend, Wilma Kirk (who was paralyzed and, in a wheelchair, as well).

Fannie Ann also went on to attend Winthrop College in Rock Hill and graduated in 1975 with a B.S. Degree in Business and from the S.C. Department of Rehabilitation in Computer Training. She also worked at Winthrop College in the education department. In addition, she was employed as a bookkeeper for Attorney Roberta Y. Wright in Rock Hill. Fannie Ann received a motorized wheelchair as a gift from her fellow students just before she graduated. Fannie Ann's dream of getting an education and attending college came true, and she was so happy about her accomplishments!

Fannie Ann's Home-Based Avon and Tax Preparation Businesses

Fannie Ann operated a home-based Avon business and a tax preparation business for many years. She started out with only a few clients, and eventually it seemed like everybody who lived in York came to her to make their Avon purchases and to have their taxes done every year. During tax season, people were in and out of the house all day long and papers were scattered everywhere! I really don't know how she kept up with all that stuff, but that was her gift and she really enjoyed it.

Fannie Ann was able to progress in her career through many people that she met, who were blessings along the way. She realized at an early age how important it was to establish genuine relationships with the many people that she met. Fannie made sure that she made such a lasting impression on people that they were able to recognize her capabilities and not her disabilities.

Fannie Ann helped me to realize and understand that no matter what hand I was dealt in life, that I could achieve so much more if I would persevere and never give up. She helped me to build my self-esteem because I was so shy and withdrawn. I remember one day when I was in school, and I came home and was feeling hurt and rejected and she wanted to know what was wrong. I told her that the kids were picking on me and looking at me funny because of my clothes. Do you know what she said? "Well, you just look back at um!" And that was her solution to my problem and that's what I did. She'd never let anyone get the best of her, not even me for that matter.

Fannie Ann—A Winner At Life

Fannie Ann was appointed to several committees and conferences by the former South Carolina Governor Dick Riley during her career. She was featured in several articles that highlighted some of the many accomplishments in her life. She didn't feel sorry for herself, and she didn't want others to feel that way either. She would be quick to let you know, "I'm just a person with a few limitations."

Another article from the Rock Hill Evening Herald dated Tuesday, August 2, 1977, described Fannie Ann as a winner at life and a woman of many talents even though she was confined to a wheelchair.

Fannie Ann was also featured in an article from the Tempo, The Carolina Magazine in Columbia, South Carolina dated Sunday, September 11, 1977, entitled "The View From a Wheelchair."

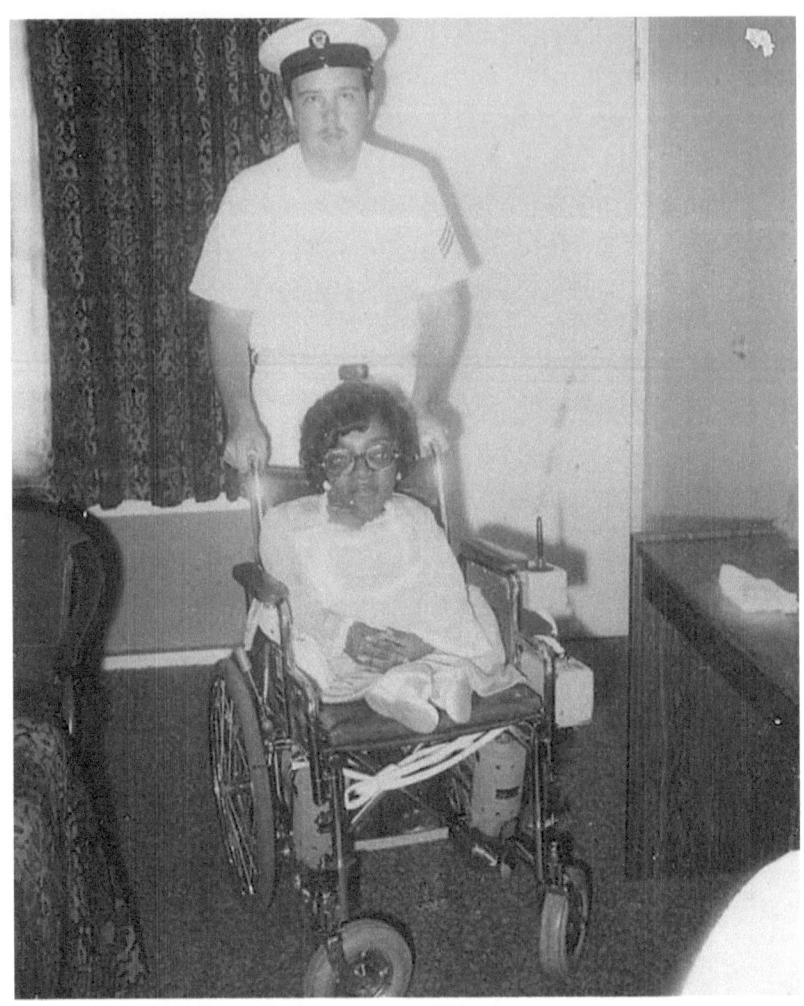

Fannie Ann and her volunteer escort from the
USS Orion docked at Charleston.

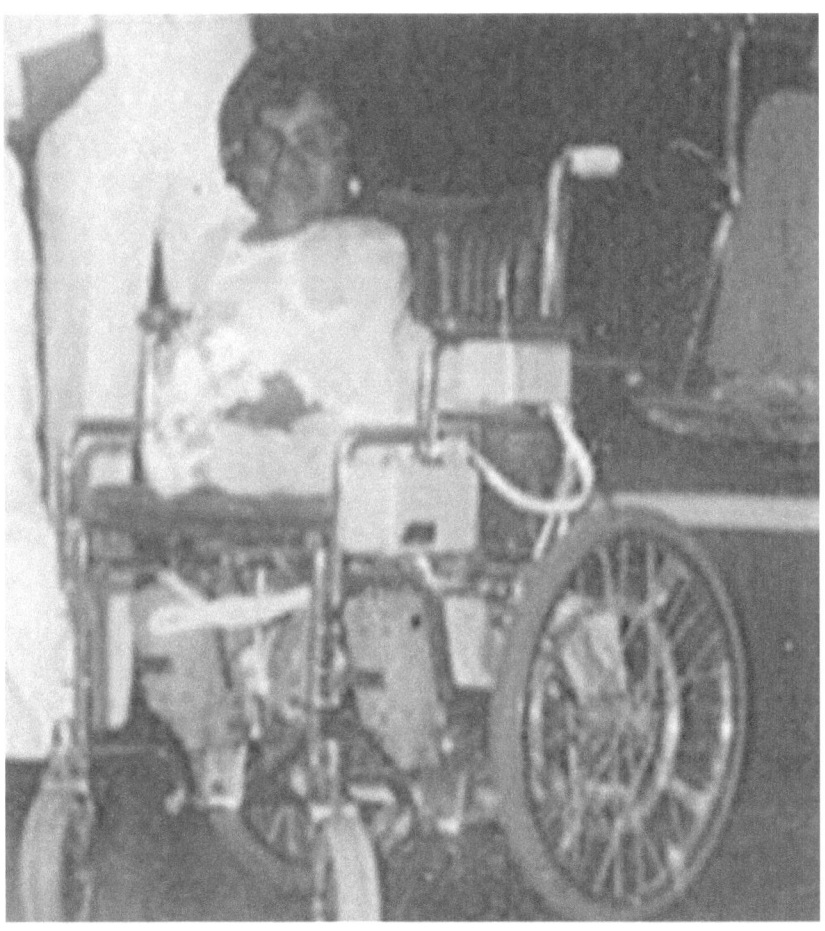

Ms. Wheelchair South Carolina pageant contestants.

*First runner-up in the 1977 Miss Wheelchair
South Carolina contest.*

In the parade in York after the wheelchair pageant with her devoted driver and caregiver, Jimmy T. Floyd.

Fannie Ann was also featured in The State Newspaper in Columbia, South Carolina dated Sunday, June 25, 1978, which celebrated Fannie Ann being crowned Ms. Wheelchair South Carolina 1979 and how she would go on to compete at the National Pageant in Columbus, Ohio.

*Fannie Ann and me when I accompanied her
to one of her meetings with Governor Dick Riley*

Fannie Ann—First in Flight

After Fannie Ann won the Ms. Wheelchair South Carolina 1978 competition at Columbia College, she went on to participate in the National Pageant in Columbus, Ohio, and I was wondering who would be able to take that long drive with her to get there. Little did I know that she was going to fly! What? Nobody else in our family had flown before that I knew of, and from what I know, she and Pearl were the first persons in the immediate family to ever fly on a plane! Fannie Ann was always ready for any type of new experience that life had to offer and embraced every opportunity that she was given.

I don't know all the details, but from what I understand, there was some type of conflict with the one of the airlines when she was supposed to be flying out to California as the airline did not want to be responsible for her because of her condition. All I know is that it was somehow resolved LEGALLY!

One thing about Fannie Ann, she was not afraid of a challenge. As a matter of fact, she seemed to thrive from them. Despite her small stature and disability, she had a great amount of faith and courage. She truly believed the scripture that says, "but with God all things are possible" (Matthew 19:26b, NIV). There were many times that I would say that I can't do something, but Fannie Ann was always quick to tell me that, "'Can't' was not in our vocabulary!" She was a great encourager and believed that she could do anything she put her mind to do.

In September 1978, Fannie Ann was featured in the Pharr Crier company newsletter, the place where I used to work which talks about how Fannie's handicap did not stopped her from getting the most out of life and highlights her winning the Miss S.C. Wheelchair title in June 1978 and from there she went on to Columbus, Ohio and won 4th place in the Miss Wheelchair America Contest.

Fannie Ann—From Labor to Reward

My dear sister had a wonderful life and she even moved into her own apartment, which was another dream that came true for her. On May 8, 1989, Fannie Ann became ill at work and remained in the hospital for four days. She never recovered and passed away from labor to reward on May 11, 1989. Although she lived only forty-three years, she accomplished more in that time than most people who live to be fifty years and older! Her homegoing service was held on May 15, 1989, and was preached by our beloved pastor, Pastor Alfred Jackson. Fannie had a very large homegoing service. The church was standing room only. Fannie Ann was well-known and loved by many people. Fannie Ann's favorite song which really reflected in her life was "Let the Life I Live Speak for Me," and her life really did speak for her.

Fannie Ann was truly an inspiration by taking advantage of every opportunity that was made available to her. Throughout her entire life, she continued to seek and embrace God and everything that God had for her. She really loved the Lord, and she followed the wonderful example that was constantly displayed by our sister, Pearl, to trust and seek God daily. Despite Fannie Ann's handicap, she was so determined to change the lives and ways of handicapped people's thinking who faced situations like hers to give them hope regardless of their situation; she persevered and encouraged others to persevere to achieve greater things in life.

CHAPTER SIX

Life in the Little City—York, SC

One of the hardest decisions I had to make was to leave Pearl and Fannie Ann and move into the city of York. I really didn't want to leave Fannie Ann because I had been responsible for taking care of her for so long. During the day, I took care of Fannie Ann who could be somewhat bossy and liked to tell us what to do. Now imagine that! I would wash and plait Fannie Ann's hair every week. When we moved with Pearl, there was lady named Mrs. Georgia Jones and her husband that lived down the hill from us and she gave me a straightening comb. I learned how to straighten hair with the hot comb. It was the kind that you had to put on the stove to get hot. I was about seven or eight years old. I remember Fannie Ann used to say, "Don't you be burning me with that straightening comb!" I learned to do my hair and I also did Pearl's and Fannie's hair.

I used to take care of her every day. As we were growing up and everybody used to go outside to play, I always wondered why she wouldn't come outside too, even though she would scoot and hustle about around the house. I could never figure it out. So, one day, I decided to pick her up and take her outside with me. We played together like we were keeping house, sweeping the yard, making mudpies and believe it or not we would plait the grass like it was hair. The whole yard would be plaited (braided)!

We spent a great deal of time together. But eventually, I moved from the country into the city with Hazel, and we moved into a house that was located near the projects on Fairview Circle.

When I first left home, I was so sad because I missed Fannie Ann so much and Hazel knew it too, so he would go get her on the weekends and let her spend the night with me. We really had some good times when she would come and stay.

When I lived in York, Hazel worked during the day at Cannon Mills. He had a house in an area in York called Johnson City where his father, John Gore, lived. Hazel rented a building near the house and that is where we ran a café and juke joint. It had a juke box, and we served fish, hamburgers and hot dogs. Hazel was the manager, and I was the cook. A lot of people used to come there throughout the day and at night. I would run the café during the day and we both would work it together at night.

Hazel rented a juke box from a man in Charlotte named Joe (Piccolo Joe) Vespoint. Joe would come down regularly to add the newest and latest records to the juke box and to service it when needed. While Piccolo Joe was servicing the jukebox, I would fix him something to eat, and he really enjoyed his meals. One day when we were talking, he said that I cooked well enough to move to Charlotte and could probably get a job at the airport. After he said that, I really thought about it long and hard. Imagine me living in Charlotte!

I met a lady by the name of Mrs. Viola Pendergrass who worked at the York Restaurant uptown, and she got me a job there as a cook. When I moved to Charlotte, Pearl was able to take over my position as a cook when I left. In 1962, before I moved to Charlotte, Hazel moved Pearl and her children into the city so that they could get back and forth to the store easily, and get to anywhere else that they needed to go. That year, Fannie Ann began high school. They moved to the east end of town in a little red house across from Hardin's Store.

CHAPTER SEVEN

Life in the Big City—Charlotte, NC

In 1961, I asked my sister Rose if I could move to Charlotte to live with her. I love her so dearly for allowing me to stay with her because she had a family already. So, I decided to move to Charlotte with my daughter, Darlene, who was born on October 10th, to live with Rose because job opportunities were limited in York at that time. My sister lived on Hill Street, about three blocks from Good Samaritan's Hospital (Good Sam's), the only black hospital in Charlotte. It was located behind Piedmont Supermarket off Remount Road which was right down the street from the famous radio station WGIV.

When I got to Charlotte, lo and behold, my sister's sister-in-law, Adeline Straite Massey, worked at the airport. She took me to the Charlotte Douglas Municipal Airport to apply for a job in the coffee shop, and I got hired on the spot. This was my first job in Charlotte working at the coffee shop at the airport bussing tables, and then I was promoted to be waitress, and I really loved it.

Although it was a very hard decision for me to leave York and especially Fannie Ann, eventually I got my driver's license and would go to York every week to get Fannie Ann. It was up and down the road for us every week. She loved coming to Charlotte on the weekends. We would ride around the city and go shopping most of the time. She always liked to be dressed up and wanted to make sure her hair and everything was in place like mine. She said that she liked that about me. She said she liked how I was always so neat and clean and well put together and said she wanted to be like me.

I had worked at the airport for about three years when I became pregnant at the age of 21 with my second child, Pamela. She was born on January 23, 1964 and shares a birthday with my sister Pearl's daughter Linda. They are one year apart and very close cousins.

My passion for cleaning and organizing continued with the first house I ever cleaned for a lady named Ms. Kirkman (I don't remember her first name). She was the supervisor at the airport coffee shop/Dobbs House, and she had a son named Holmer Jr. The Dobbs House was a place where they had big fancy parties for the important people that would come to town. Also, we catered for the airplanes. When Holmer Jr. opened a restaurant called the Golden Eagle Restaurant in downtown Charlotte, Mrs. Kirkman sent me there to help him out, but it was with the understanding that if I did not like it, I could come back with her because I was one of her best workers. I worked at the Golden Eagle with Holmer Jr. for two years and eventually went back to the airport because I had been working split shifts and it interfered with Hazel's work schedule since he had to pick me up. I didn't yet have my driver's license. There were only three blacks working there at the time, and I was the only black waitress working out front. I did well there, and I never experienced any racism or discrimination or ever felt out of place there. The people were very nice, and the tips were great.

*Photo of me at work in the brochure from the
Golden Eagle Restaurant in downtown Charlotte*

I continued to work at the airport for eleven years. I met a lot of people there and will be forever grateful to Adeline for inspiring me. We truly had some great times working together there. That TV show "Scandal" ain't got nothing on the "Scandal at the Charlotte Douglas Municipal Airport!"

After I had my kids, I always saved some money when I started working because I knew that I could not ask Pearl or anybody else for money. So, I did my best to be responsible, make good decisions and not spend all my money.

I stayed with my sister Rose for about a year, and then I got my own apartment on Wigg Street off South Tryon behind the old Piedmont Supermarket. At that point, Hazel relocated to Charlotte. When he joined me, we moved again to Bank Street.

One day I started thinking that we needed a home for our children because I did not want to live in an apartment anymore. So, I started riding around with my daughters in the car and saw this house that I really liked. It was everything that I imagined that I wanted in a home. I wrote down the address and phone number and called the realtor whose name was Neal Wilkerson. A couple of days later, he agreed to show us the house and allowed me to apply for it and said that he had called my job for references. He also mentioned that someone else had applied for it as well. However, a couple of days later, he called and said that I was approved for the loan. He called my boss, Bill Ward, and he told him to let me have anything I wanted because I was a good worker. On August 17, 1967, I was able to purchase our first home and have been there ever since. I have been in that same house for fifty years. Purchasing a home was a major accomplishment, and that made it possible for me to be a blessing to many people!

Out at a party. Hazel loved to party and dance!

Getting ready to go out on the town.

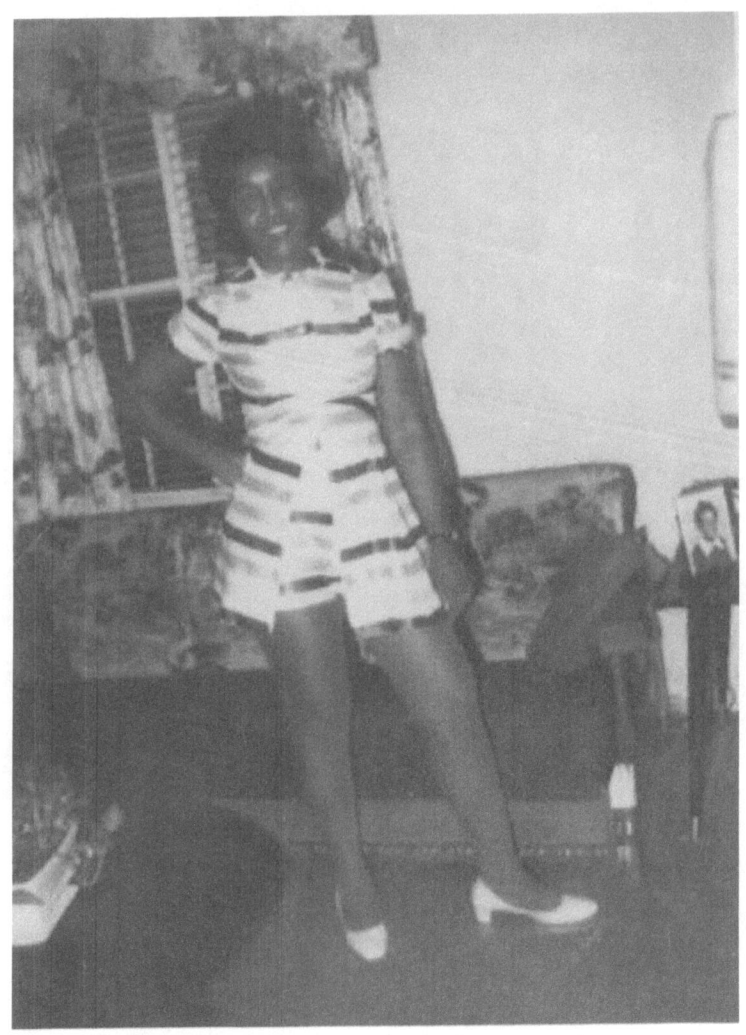

Getting ready to go out to the hot pants dance.

Hazel, the children (Darlene and Pam) and me

Darlene (Doll) and Pam with Hazel's boat

Darlene and Pam hanging out with Hazel

Hazel and me

In 1966 when I was living on Bank Street, I met a special woman named Ms. Creola Robinson who worked for the Charlotte Area Fund. She became a godmother to me, and my children became her grandchildren. She would come around to the apartments for business regarding the Charlotte Area Fund. We began to talk a lot and became friends through our many, many talks. She fell in love with my two children. She exposed them to as many positive things in life that she could. She put Pam in ballet classes, took them to see plays and attended many different types of events and shows. She took Darlene on her first trip to Disney World. She helped me understand so many things in life, such as how to present myself at fancy affairs. She taught me how to dress appropriately for those fancy occasions - what to wear, what not wear, and when to wear it. Back then, you had certain types of jewelry you wore to daytime events and occasions and evening affairs.

Living in a big city was so much different than living in the small town of York. Ms. Robinson taught me a lot of things in life that I never knew. When I was young, I had low self-esteem; I felt like I wasn't good enough to be around certain types of well-educated, well-to-do folks. Creola encouraged me by letting me know that I was just as good as anybody else. She said that just because someone may be a doctor or a lawyer, or someone may be rich, it did not matter. I was just as good, and my education did not matter. Creola reminded me that we are all God's children and that I was important too.

Creola was a great cook. She would cook and prepare catered meals for doctors and lawyers when they went up to the mountains every year, and I would go and help her. She would cater the food and clean up afterwards. Creola taught me so much about how to carry myself on those jobs and how to present myself at the fancy affairs we catered.

She would always say, "You go in as a woman of respect and come out as a woman with respect and do your job well. You will be okay wherever you go and whatever you do in life. People will return that respect, and they won't say just anything to you or around you." Creola Robinson was my rock. She spoke her mind; she did not take any mess from anyone, and she was a woman of her word.

Creola adopted us as her family because she did not have any children of her own. She wanted only the best for my children. She picked them up from school when I was working at Pharr Yarns in McAdenville, North Carolina on second shift. She encouraged them to get involved in activities, ballet, playing instruments, arts and travel because she loved to travel. She used to travel all over the world. She had been to places like Spain, Japan and China. China was her last big trip because she always said that she wanted to go to the Great Wall of China, and she did! She took both of my children on their first trip to Disney World in Florida.

We stayed friends until she passed away at the age of 82 on April 22, 1988.

Creola Robinson. She was such a great godmother

*Me getting ready to go out to an event with Creola
at the White House Inn in downtown Charlotte*

Hazel and me at Creola's house

CHAPTER EIGHT

Still Looking for a Better Life

A s I mentioned before, I decided to go back to the airport because the split shift at the Golden Eagle did not work out so well. From there I went to Pharr Yarns in Belmont, North Carolina and I worked there for eleven years, and I was making more money. Eventually I left there and began a part-time job working for ServiceMaster Building Maintenance Services. My supervisor's name was Dan Coblenz. I was the supervisor over the cleaning crew on this job for about ten years.

Later, I went out on my own and became self-employed cleaning houses and continued to provide janitorial services for one office building. I worked in the houses during the day and in the building at night. Cooking and cleaning were my specialties and my gift, and I loved doing these two things the most out of all my job experiences. I was most happy and at peace doing this, and I did both very well. As time went on, I got jobs cleaning many of the finest homes in the Queen City of Charlotte. At one time, I worked for three doctors - one dentist, one gynecologist, and one pediatric heart specialist.

Key Realty of Charlotte was my first contract building where I worked on my own for Joseph Vandevere, his wife Diane, and his sister Sandra Burke. Key Realty was one of the most well-known real estate agencies in Charlotte. They were wonderful people to work for and were a great blessing to me during the time that I worked for their family. All of them treated me extremely well and were always willing to do whatever they could to assist me in any way. After Hazel died, they were there to support me with the upkeep of my home. Sandra and her husband, Clint, would come by and assist me with odd jobs that I had around the house. They were always only a phone call away. They were like my family. I also had the opportunity to clean their homes as well as enjoyed going fishing at their homes on the lake.

Over the years, sometimes my children were able to help me out in my cleaning business, and for the most part they worked well because they knew that I wouldn't have it any other way. I made it clear to them to that they could either do their job well, or they could go!

On my journey, I was blessed to work for many different employers which included Mrs. Kirkman (airport coffee shop/owner/operator), whom I mentioned earlier. Although I worked for her at the airport, I also cleaned her house. I would leave work from the airport about 1:00 p.m., and she would take me to her house on Scaleybark to clean and then take me home. I worked for her for about four years, and it was a pleasure working for her.

I also had the pleasure of working for a lady by the name of Shirley and her husband, Peter. Shirley was a very special lady. She lived not far from the Raintree area. We got along great and had a great relationship. She worked at the Ivey's Department Stores, and she traveled a lot to different cities to set up displays for Estee Lauder products in all the Ivey's stores. Shirley and I were the same size, and she made sure she kept me supplied with clothes, shoes and handbags. After many years, the Ivey's stores closed, and she and her family moved to Florida. We are still in contact today; she sends pictures and letters often. We had some great times together and we hosted some great parties together. They were very good friends as well. They were a blessing from the Lord to me, and I had the privilege to visit them in Florida in 2015.

During the time that I worked at my night cleaning job for ServiceMaster, I met a woman by the name of Carolyn. I know that God placed her in my life. Carolyn was instrumental in assisting me with financial matters when necessary.

Carolyn introduced me to her sister, Maggie and her husband Greg, and oh what another great blessing they have been to me throughout the years! Greg would assist me with my garden by putting up stakes for my tomatoes, and they did well. At first, I started working for Maggie and then she introduced me to several of her good friends as well. They all treated me very, very well through various acts of kindness. For example, if I needed any repairs at my home, they would help with that. If I had a need, all I had to do was ask and they were more than willing to help me out. They always blessed me well during the holidays. They were very loving and caring employers.

I met a lady named Susan and her husband David. They had two children, John and Annie, and we became very close. She was like a sister to me. She was such a blessing to me in so many ways when I needed resource assistance with health issues. Her children would come and spend weekends at my house and play with my granddaughter, and they really had a great time together. Although I was no longer working for them, they would always send cards at Christmas time, visit and bring homemade rum cake!

I also had the pleasure to meet and work for Jean and Vickie. They have also contributed to my life. They ensured that I my needs were met, and I could never thank them enough for their kindness and generosity to me and my family!

I am thankful to have had the opportunity to work in some of the most exclusive homes in York and Charlotte. These neighborhoods included homes in River Hills, Lake Wylie, Scaleybark, Raintree, SouthPark, Carmel Road, Providence, Queens Road, Dilworth and Myers Park.

CHAPTER NINE

Time to Worship

When I first moved to Charlotte to stay with my sister, Rose, I had not found a place to attend church that was within walking distance to where she lived, and I did not have my driver's license at that time. I knew sooner or later I would need to find a church where I could take time to worship. When I moved to an apartment that was between Wigg and Annette Streets right off Remount Road, I found a church that was within walking distance that I attended – Temple Chapel Baptist Church. I knew that it was very important to make sure that my children were trained in the things of the Lord just like Pearl had taught me to do. She always emphasized that I needed to always put God first in everything that I did. Temple Chapel was within walking distance from where I lived on Bank Street as well. I liked going there because it reminded me so much of our home church. The singing and foot stomping when they sang hymns made me feel right at home, and the people were nice and welcoming as well.

I continued to worship there until I met Creola Robinson, and then I started going to church with her at Amy James Presbyterian Church that was located on West Boulevard. It was not far from our house. My children used to go to vacation bible school there and were able to walk there because it was that close to the house. The Presbyterian Church was so much different from the Baptist church. They sang from the hymn books, but they were quieter and more reserved. You didn't make all the foot stomping noise in there! I believe I stayed there until Creola passed away and then decided to go back to my home church in South Carolina since it was only thirty-two miles away.

When Hazel got to the point that he was no longer able to make the trip to York every Sunday due to his failing health, we decided to stay at home and would visit when we could. Later, we had a group of church members that lived in Charlotte who went from house to house that would have Bible study and prayer meetings each week, and we participated in those meetings with them. We enjoyed some great times of praise, worship and fellowship at the house. What I enjoyed the most was the singing of those old hymns. My favorite hymn is Amazing Grace. I get so happy whenever I hear anybody singing that song. My favorite scripture is Psalms 27:1a (KJV), "The Lord is my light and my salvation; whom shall I fear?" That scripture has brought me so much comfort and peace many times in my life.

Nowadays, I attend church with my daughter occasionally when I feel up to it, and I'm still trusting, believing and thanking God daily!

CHAPTER TEN

Through It All—Celebrating Life

I have suffered the loss of many loved ones over the years, but through it all, God has continued to be faithful and good to me and my family. On Father's Day, Sunday, June 20, 1993, I lost my beloved, Hazel. For thirty-six years, Hazel and I were able to enjoy many wonderful experiences, and for this I am truly grateful to God. After Hazel passed away, I felt so lost and alone because I had been with him most of my life. He was my "knight in shining armor." I can truly say that my faith in God is what really helped me get through that difficult time in my life - but I can tell you that it was not easy.

My family and I have had many glorious celebrations which included the birth of my children and grandchildren, birthday parties, weddings, anniversaries, graduations and school accomplishments. I have traveled to many places in my life and have had the opportunity to take yearly summer vacations with my family to the beach.

I have had the pleasure to enjoy several cruises to the Bahamas that were afforded to me by my dear and faithful son-in-law, Earl Barnett. Earl has been a tremendous blessing in providing for me in any and every way that he can. Every day he calls to make sure I'm okay and checks to see if I need anything done. All I need to do is let him know and he makes sure my request is fulfilled without hesitation or delay. Earl always goes above and beyond the call of duty, and I am truly blessed and grateful to have him in my life!

Me and my son-in-law, Earl

I have tried to keep my sister Pearl's legacy alive by taking care of many relatives and friends by allowing them to come and live with us in order to attend school or college, to work at jobs that they may have had in Charlotte, or by having them come to live with us whenever necessary to help them get on their feet. I have also had the privilege and pleasure of relatives and friends to come and babysit for us or spend their summer vacations to hang out with the kids at the Revolution Park and Swimming Pool. Some would work with Hazel to make money cutting grass, hauling cardboard, or picking up beer cans. It was like a rotating shift of relatives from York, Charlotte, High Point, Washington, D.C., or wherever!

Below is a list of the individuals that we enjoyed and with whom we shared our home or whom we "adopted" into our family:

Cindy Alvord	Jerron Johnson
Maurice Kennedy Berry	Quittie Johnson
Deaner Bratton	Veronica Johnson
Jimmy Brown	Hazel Kennedy Jones
Tony Brown	Evon Kennedy
Debra Burris	Lonnie Jermaine Kennedy
Raynette Giles Clark	Lonnie John Kennedy
Jerrica Cole	Minnie Bryant Kennedy
Andre Currence	Terrence Kennedy
Sarah Dickson	Brian Lewis
Diane Floyd	Angela Marrow
Jimmy T. Floyd	Almeta Perkins
Ronnie Floyd	Andre Owens
Diana Giles	Annie Perkins
Arthur (Taxi) Gill	Barry Perkins
James (Danny Boy) Gill	Benny Perkins
Joann (Punkin) Gill	Levander (Butt Nose) Perkins
Linda Gill	James Rush
Nancy Gill	Larry Rush
Flora "LeeLee" Gore	Legwenia Rush
Gordon (Bo Jap) Gore	Willie Woody
John Robert Gore	Monica Wright
Tavares Kennedy Hall	

Nowadays the house is not as busy as it used to be, and when I am not working, I spend my time in my vegetable garden along with my devoted and faithful godson, James Rush. Through his total commitment, James ensures that everything around my home is always in tip-top shape. I place most of the foods I grow in canning jars such as green beans, tomatoes (soup), cucumbers, squash, okra, peppers, and cabbage, and I give them to people for Christmas and birthdays. I also have a lot of flowers that I cultivate because I seem to have a green thumb. Many of my flowers look just as good as the flowers in the flower shops. I still enjoy baking cakes and cooking (every Sunday) for my family and friends whenever they stop by. I still enjoy fishing when I can.

Me and my godson, James Rush

Just a few family members and godchildren

In conclusion, I must say that the journey has truly been great, and to God be the glory for the things He has done! Despite any circumstances that you may face in life, you must persevere, and if you trust and believe in God and follow your dreams, you can make it in life.

SO MANY BLESSINGS ALONG THE WAY

END

References

Chapter 1: Sharecropping: Definition and Dates – HISTORY. (2010, June 24). *HISTORY.*

https://www.history.com/topics/black–history/sharecropping

Contact The Author

Georgia Bell Floyd Kennedy
Phone: +1 (704) 332-8735